WAFFEN-SS in the West

WAFFEN-SS in the West

Holland, Belgium, France 1940

A Documentary in Photos
by SS War Correspondent Friedrich Zschäckel, SS-PK

Edited by Michael D. Beaver
with Gunther Vorreiter and David Krakow

Schiffer Military History
Atglen, PA

Library of Congress Catalog Number: 2001096729.

Printed in China.
ISBN: 0-7643-1553-6

Published by Schiffer Publishing Ltd.
4880 Lower Valley Road
Atglen, PA 19310
Phone: (610) 593-1777
FAX: (610) 593-2002
E-mail: Schifferbk@aol.com.
Visit our web site at: www.schifferbooks.com
Please write for a free catalog.
This book may be purchased from the publisher.
Please include $3.95 postage.
Try your bookstore first.

In Europe, Schiffer books are distributed by:
Bushwood Books
6 Marksbury Ave.
Kew Gardens
Surrey TW9 4JF
England
Phone: 44 (0)208 392-8585
FAX: 44 (0)208 392-9876
E-mail: Bushwd@aol.com.
Free postage in the UK. Europe: air mail at cost.
Try your bookstore first.

Foreword

The fast, irresistible advance in the West, and the forced march through Holland, Belgium, and France, has given us a different picture and viewpoint. Our inspiration came from our recollections and images of the previous World War. The tactics of the National Socialist Revolution and its new army gave war a new face: the vast and great emptiness of the battlefield.

The human being, the man stands again in the focus, after visionless prophets had predicted the subtle material-battles following the style of the last World War. The individual man, equipped with the best weapons, deeply affected and led by fierce faith, strengthened by best and clear persuasion, he is the bearer of victory, he is the spirit of battle.

In him, in his face, in his attitude, in running, in jumping, in exhaustion and utmost concentration, the great fierce days of permanent attack, the power, the force and sublime certainty are reflected. Everything else around him is mostly background, the wide stage of this solemn play.

The war correspondents of the Waffen-SS, soldiers of our fast divisions, carried along with themselves, in addition to their weapons, in long hot marches, in battles and attacks, their sense of simple duty for the ordinary experienced individual. Thereby helping to create the big picture of the National Socialist soldier. They gave their lives as fighters of a young armed force. They demonstrated to themselves and to the regiments of the Waffen-SS, that they did not aspire to be something better than the infantrymen, the anti-tank men, or the artillery men, not more, but also never less.

In my company, several good war correspondents performed their duties. If we collected only the photographs from a single SS war correspondent company, and used these to create a picture of this part of the war, then only because from the very beginning the correspondent put the individual man, his face, his attitude in action, to be the focus of his work, that he achieved, without demand for perfection, the true reflection for the German fight for freedom.

This series of photos was taken during the battles of one division of the Waffen-SS in the West. Like other parts of the Waffen-SS with their regiments, they went through fierce weeks in the East. So this division, fighting and victorious as the other divisions and regiments of the Waffen-SS, originated from a common nucleus, and energized by the same motivation.

These pictures shall bear witness of the young soldiers of the German revolution, who faithfully gave their best in the great victorious army, and lived under the motto given by Adolf Hitler to his bodyguards during the hardest times: "SS-man, your honor is loyalty."

The book shall be, at the same time, a monument for the honor of the truest. Their bodies rest in foreign soil, their life is with us and leads above the flags and standards of the regiments forward to eternal German victory in war and peace.

Gunther d'Alquen
In the Field, February 1941.

The face of the Waffen-SS

Mechanized troops

Reconnaissance troops are behind the enemy for days

The advance guard riders...

...always in the saddle

The situation will be announced

"The column marches here!"

Forward on endless streets

Battalion headquarters

Early morning and the rooster crows

In the assembly point

Holland ...

... on narrow causeways through flooded land

Shortly before contact with the enemy

Now the group is compact

Ammunition carrier

Machinegun crew

The heavy MG

Across from the enemy

Now the Air force moves in

The division-commander

That was one day!

Rushing over the dam

The forest is mopped up

The foxhole

I had...

...a comrade

After a quick thrust, the last house is reached

The advance guard

Our youth

On an ambush

The village will be combed through

Street under fire

An anti-tank cannon is in front

The platoon leader

And now – the rush!

Catch a short breath

Anti-tank cannon without motorization

...but with men...

...preparation...

...move right...

…fire…

...and a hit

Dangerous handwork

The victor

Direct hit!

Into position, move!

Infantry...infantry!

Hot days...

...hot nights

That was in Aire

Mobile cover

With and...

... behind the tanks

Farther, always farther

The company troops

Look out, what…

...is going on up front?

The vehicles are left behind

The assault troops

Don't make a sound!

The order is carried out, assemble!

Officer, non-commissioned officer, and enlisted man

A delay

Before a great cause

When does it start?

Districts and...

... the countryside are mopped up!

The commanding officer makes an assignment

Away from cover

The patrol leader

Battalions adjutant is wounded

Punctual as always, our Stukas

Meter by meter...

...the company crawls...

...in anticipation of the decisive moments

Short rest

The line of fire has moved forward

Objective is reached!

Now the artillery gets the word.

The front line soldier in 1940

Sleep is important...

...as ammunition

Good camouflage is half of the battle

On the move again soon

And then the Pioneers

Over the Schelde, the Maus, and the Rhein

Water is...

...no hindrance

On other shores

A bridge here quickly!

Protective cover fire

The observer

Over the open field

Corporal and enlisted man

A pause in the struggle

The sergeant

It isn't half as bad!

The doctor brings you back

Once more things went well

Each one was found

Where are the Tommies

Dismounted

A quick swallow

Support, support!

Soldier and reporter…

...war correspondent

Down off the bikes now!

The anti-tank cannon is brought forward

One hundred meter ditch by the road...

...seems like a mile wide

Forward, forward!

Yet the blessing comes from above

As practiced a thousand times

Yet many a man remain behind

Caution, this stinks

Pursuit

Resistance in the town...

...is soon broken

The motorcycle messenger

"Get going!"

ϟϟ-4504
4

Between two assignments

For this there is little time

The long arm of the infantry

Shot fired!

The artillery of the small men

The messenger must come right away

Provide for yourself

Only a few lines

For fulfilling duty

"...we march, we march along into France!"